PEGASUS ENCYCLOPEDIA LIBRARY

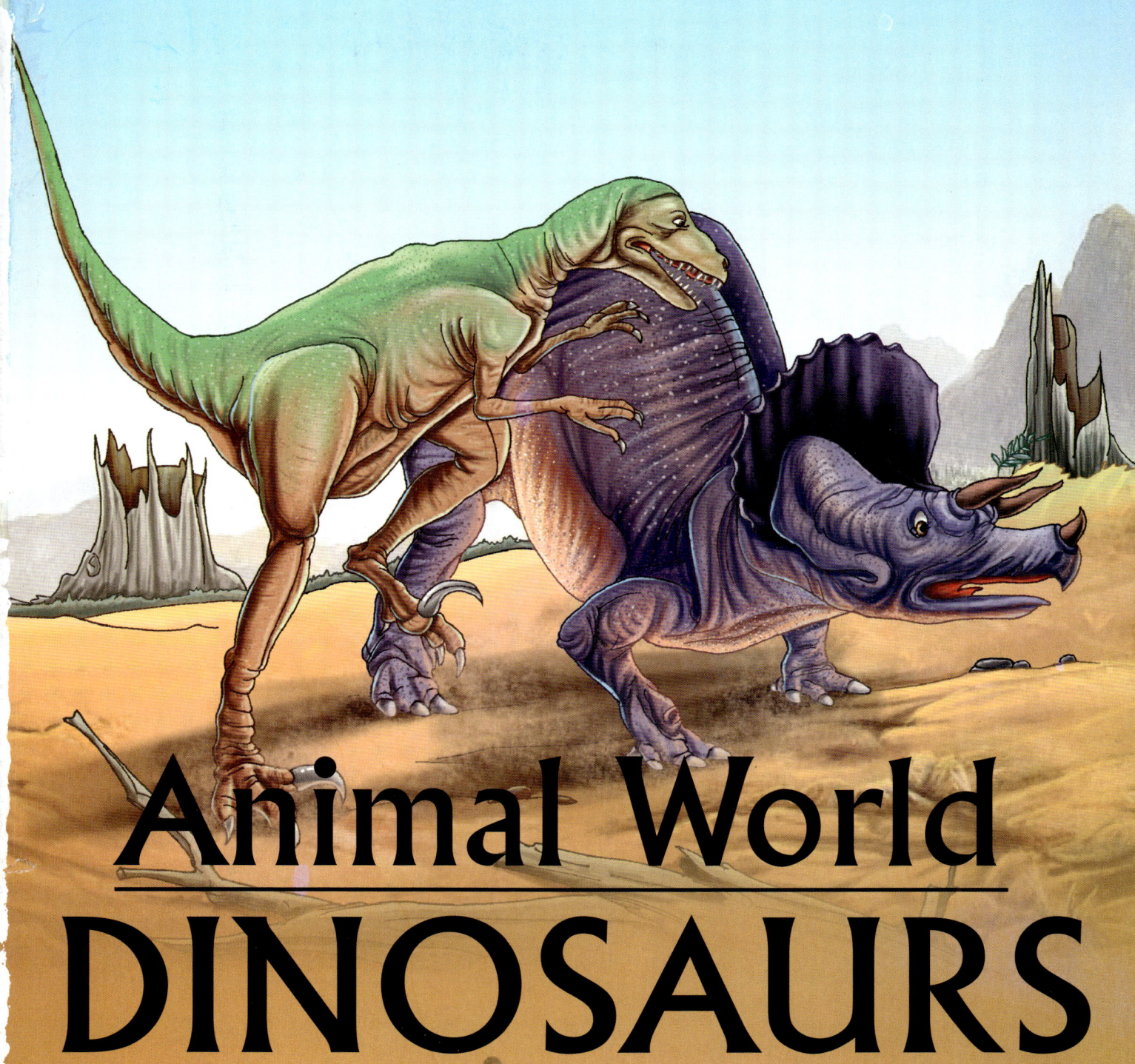

Animal World
DINOSAURS

Edited by: Pallabi B. Tomar, Hitesh Iplani
Managing editor: Tapasi De
Designed by: Vijesh Chahal, Anil kumar, Rohit Kumar
Illustrated by: Suman S. Roy, Tanoy Choudhury
Colouring done by: Vinay Kumar, Kiran Kumari & Pradeep Kumar

CONTENTS

What are dinosaurs? 3

Evolution of dinosaurs 4

Where did dinosaurs live? 7

How did dinosaurs move? 8

Size of the dinosaurs 9

What colour were the dinosaurs? 10

Food habits 11

Dinosaur behaviour 14

Extinction 17

Dinosaur fossils 20

Dinosaur extremes 22

Some well-known dinosaurs 24

Test Your Memory 31

Index 32

What are dinosaurs?

The term 'dinosaur' originates from the Greek words 'deino' and 'sauros', meaning 'terrible' and 'lizard'.

Sir Richard Owen invented the name 'dinosaur' in 1842, to describe an extinct group of reptiles that lived during the Mesozoic period. Dinosaurs are animals that dominated the world for over 100-million years. We come to know about them from fossils including fossilized bones, feathers, impressions of skin and internal organs and soft tissues, including blood vessels and cells lining them.

Dinosaurs have become a part of the world culture, and have remained consistently popular, especially among children. They have been featured in bestselling books and blockbuster films like Jurassic Park and new discoveries about them are regularly covered by the media.

> The first dinosaur bones were discovered in 1822 in Sussex, England, by Gideon Mantell. It was a herbivore (plant eating) dinosaur later given the name, Iguanodon.

Evolution of dinosaurs

The evolution of dinosaurs is a passage through nearly 350 million years in the history of the planet Earth. The various geological periods mentioned below represent the divisions of geological time through which the evolution of the dinosaurs and their ancestors can be traced.

The triassic period
(about 250 to 210 million years ago)

The evolution of the archosaurs and early dinosaurs

During the Triassic period, all the continents of the Earth were joined together to form a supercontinent called **Pangaea**. As the continent was so large, much of the interior was a long distance from the sea, which resulted in very dry and hot climates. The first dinosaurs were to appear in the late Triassic. In the Early Triassic, however, land ecosystems were dominated by the immediate ancestors of the dinosaurs, the archosaurs.

During the Triassic, the carnivorous dinosaurs such as the sleek **Coelophysis** and the larger and more robust **Herrerasaurus** occupied an important position previously occupied by the carnivorous **archosaurs**. Others showed an evolutionary trend towards greater size, such as the **Plateosaurus** and became adapted to an herbivorous diet.

The first dinosaur to be named was Megalosaurus. It was named in 1824 by Reverend William Buckland.

The jurassic period
(about 210 to 150 million years ago)

Dinosaurs dominate the land

During the Jurassic period, the supercontinent Pangaea was beginning to break up due to the mechanisms of plate tectonics. This allowed narrow seaways to spread between the continents, but land links still existed that allowed the dinosaurs to spread throughout the continent. The extinction of the mammal-like reptiles at the Triassic-Jurassic merging boundaries allowed the dinosaurs to diversify rapidly in the early Jurassic.

The mild Jurassic climate (though still warm) allowed the largest dinosaurs to evolve. The early sauropods continued into the Jurassic and showed an increase in size. The 10 m long sauropod **Vulcanodon** showed numerous changes in the skeletal structure to accommodate the great increase in weight. This animal laid the foundation for the true dinosaur giants which evolved early in the Jurassic and became distributed worldwide. From these animals, more advanced sauropods such as **Brachiosaurus** evolved, which had a very long neck and elongated forelimbs, an adaptation to reach high vegetation. Other sauropods were adapted to browsing on lower vegetation. The largest of all sauropods also belong to the Jurassic age.

The largest carnivore of the early Jurassic was the double-crested **Dilophosaurus** which was up to 6m in length.

> **Astonishing fact**
> At present over 1,000 different species of dinosaur have been identified and named.

The cretaceous period
(about 150 to 65 million years ago)

The greatest diversity of dinosaurs

By the Cretaceous, the distribution of the continents was nearly done and the continents were becoming more similar to the present day. The climate was very warm, the Atlantic Ocean opened and the seaways were more extensive. The separation of landmasses isolated certain groups of dinosaurs and allowed them to evolve separately from each other. This isolation allowed the tremendous diversity of Cretaceous dinosaurs to evolve.

The large sauropods of the Jurassic were rare, however. The majority of the herbivores that replaced them were smaller dinosaurs which showed a greater diversity of form, the ornithopods. The replacement of the sauropods by the ornithopods probably reflects the influence of environmental stresses on the large sauropods. Perhaps the large sauropods had some difficulty in adapting to a diet of flowering plants that evolved in the Cretaceous. Iguanodon was the largest of the ornithopods, and in the early Cretaceous evolved a wide variety of specialisations related to its diet.

During the late Cretaceous, the largest terrestrial carnivores of all evolved such as the Tyrannosaurus. Also at this time the 'duck-billed' dinosaurs came to prominence. The well-known horned dinosaurs, such as Triceratops evolved from the beaked, early Cretaceous Psittacosaurus. The elaborate horn development may have served as a defensive weapon, a signalling device or may have been used during rutting contests, similar to the antlers of modern deer.

Did you know that most dinosaurs were vegetarians?

Where did dinosaurs live?

Palaeontologists, the scientists who study fossils, now have evidence that dinosaurs lived on all the continents. At the beginning of the age of dinosaurs (during the Triassic Period, about 230 million years ago) the continents we now know were arranged together as a single supercontinent called Pangaea. During the 165 million years of dinosaur existence this supercontinent slowly broke apart. Its pieces then spread across the globe into a nearly modern arrangement by a process called plate tectonics. Volcanoes, earthquakes, mountain building and sea-floor spreading are all part of plate tectonics and this process is still changing our modern Earth. As Pangaea broke apart, dinosaurs became scattered across the globe on separate continents, and new types of dinosaurs evolved separately in each geographic area.

Dinosaur communities were separated by both time and geography. The 'age of dinosaurs' (the Mesozoic Era) included three consecutive geologic time periods (the Triassic, Jurassic, and Cretaceous Periods). Different dinosaur species lived during each of these three periods. For example, the Jurassic dinosaur Stegosaurus already had been extinct for approximately 80 million years before

the appearance of the Cretaceous dinosaur Tyrannosaurus. In fact, the time separating Stegosaurus and Tyrannosaurus is greater than the time separating Tyrannosaurus and the humans.

After the dinosaurs died out, nearly 65 million years passed before people appeared on Earth. However, small mammals were alive at the time of the dinosaurs.

> The oldest known dinosaur is Eoraptor, a meat-eater that lived 228 million years ago.

DINOSAURS

How did dinosaurs move?

Dinosaurs usually walked on their toes. Some dinosaurs moved around on four legs (quadrupeds) and some on two legs (bipeds). Others may have run on two legs but walked and grazed on all four legs. Some dinosaurs were slow moving and others were speedy, depending on their structure. A few of the late, bird-like dinosaurs may have used their short, feathered arms to help speed up their running and perhaps glide from trees to the ground. Dinosaurs probably used their tails for balance while moving and some may have used their tails for quickly shifting their balance during quick turns.

Huge dinosaurs with short legs, like Apatosaurus, Diplodocus, Brachiosaurus, and the other sauropods, were probably among the slowest of the dinosaurs.

The speediest dinosaurs were the bird-like, bipedal carnivores with long, slim hind-limbs and light bodies. These fast dinosaurs probably weren't any faster than modern-day land animals. For example, Ornithomimus was a fast, agile dinosaur, probably running about as quickly as an ostrich, which can run up to 70 kph.

Most dinosaurs hatched from eggs and they could not fly or live in water.

Size of the dinosaurs

Dinosaurs ranged in size from the size of a chicken to well over 100 ft long. Most dinosaurs were somewhere in the middle. The modern-day blue whale is the largest animal that ever lived. It is larger than any dinosaur was.

No one knows why some of the dinosaurs became so huge. This is one of the most interesting unanswered questions in palaeontology. Palaeontologists don't know for certain, but perhaps a large body size protected them from most predators, helped to regulate internal body temperature or let them reach new sources of food (some probably browsed treetops, as giraffes do today). No modern animals except whales are even close in size to the largest dinosaurs; therefore, palaeontologists think that the dinosaurs' world was much different from the world today and that climate and food supplies must have been favourable for reaching great size.

Astonishing fact

The biggest dinosaurs were over 100 ft long and 50 ft tall!

What colour were the dinosaurs?

The colour of the dinosaur skin is not clearly known from the fossils. Palaeontologists think that some dinosaurs likely had protective coloration, such as pale undersides to reduce shadows, irregular colour patterns to make them less visible in vegetation and so on. Those dinosaurs that had enough armour, such as the stegosaurs and ceratopsians, may not have needed protective coloration but may have been brightly coloured as a warning to predators or as a display for finding a mate. Most dinosaurs probably were as brightly coloured as modern lizards, snakes, or birds.

The largest of dinosaurs (like the giant sauropods) were probably neutral-coloured or grey, like the largest animals today (example elephants). No one knows of what colours or patterns most of the dinosaurs were. Most likely, dinosaurs that were hunted for their meat were camouflaged in order to hide somewhat from the predators, coloured in a particular fashion to attract mates or brightly coloured to let predators know that they tasted awful! Different colours are also important where temperature regulation is concerned. They absorb or reflect sunlight as the animal controls its body temperature.

Fossilized skin impressions have only been found for a small fraction of the known dinosaurs. Not much is known about dinosaur skin and there is some debate among palaeontologists about this topic. Most skin fossils show bumpy skin, not scaly skin. Only the huge plant-eaters seem to have had scaly skin.

Astonishing fact

Dinosaurs probably lived to be between 75 to 300 years of age!

Food habits

Some dinosaurs were carnivores but most were herbivores. This is true for all animal populations. In any food chain, there have to be more organisms at the lower levels of the chain because the transfer of food energy is inefficient and much of the energy is lost at each stage of the process.

A large number of plants (called producers or autotrophs) can support a smaller number of plant-eaters (called primary consumers). These plant-eaters are eaten by a smaller number of carnivores (secondary consumers).

For example, it may have taken hundreds of acres of plants to feed a small group of Triceratops. These Triceratops could supply a single T. Rex with enough food to survive over its lifetime.

Astonishing fact

Quetzalcoatlus is named after the winged Aztec god Quetzalcoatl. This gigantic pterosaur had a wingspan of up to 45 ft, making it the largest creature ever to fly.

Roughly 65 percent of the dinosaurs were plant eaters and 35 percent were meat-eaters or omnivores. If you look at the number of actual fossils found, the percentage of plant-eaters increases, since many fossils of the plant-eaters have been found. For example, over a hundred Protoceratops fossils have been found, but only about a dozen Tyrannosaurus fossils have been found.

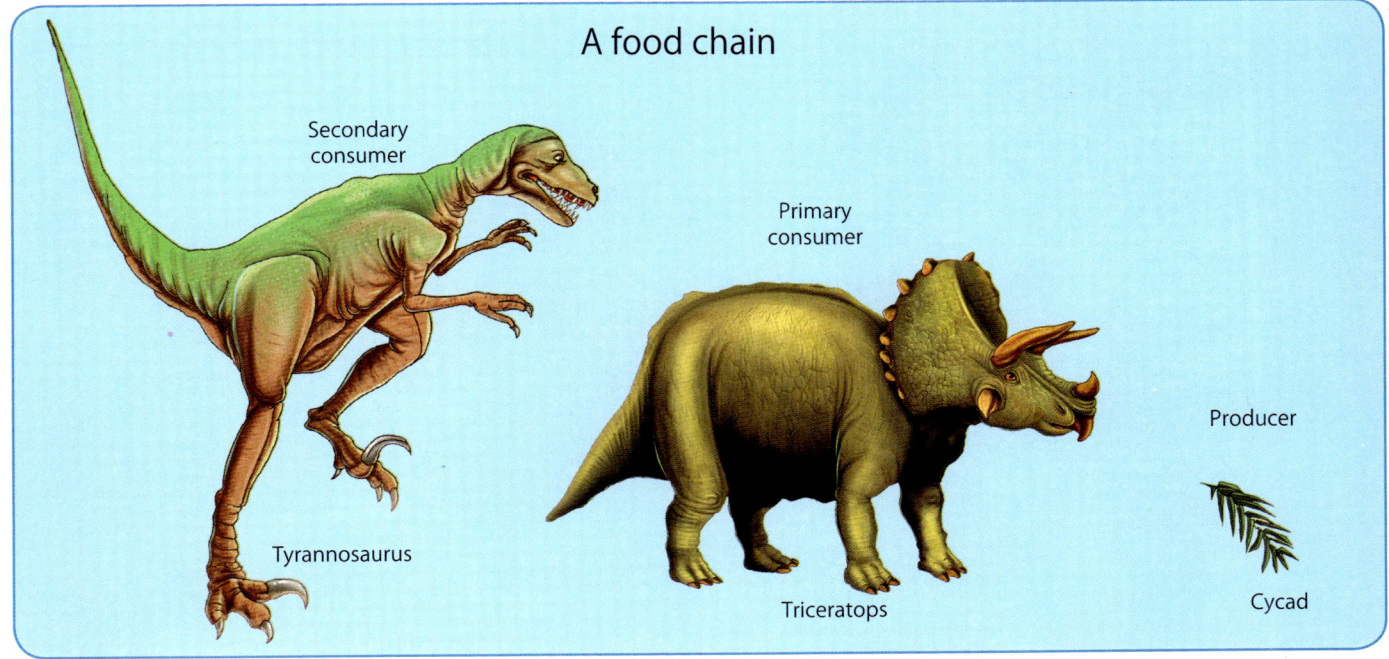

A food chain

As the number of carnivores in a community increases, they eat more and more of the herbivores, decreasing the herbivore population. It then becomes harder and harder for the carnivores to find herbivores to eat, and the population of carnivores decreases. In this way, the carnivores and herbivores stay in a relatively stable equilibrium, each limiting the others population. A similar equilibrium exists between plants and plant-eaters.

Herbivores

Plant-eaters or herbivores usually have blunt teeth that are good for stripping vegetation (leaves, twigs, etc.). Some also have flat teeth for grinding tough plant fibres. Many herbivores have cheek pouches in which they can store food for a while.

Plant-eaters usually have to eat a much larger volume of material than meat-eaters do in order to get the same amount of calories (this is because leaves, twigs, and roots are low in calories). Plant-eaters usually have larger digestive systems (than meat-eaters) that are needed to digest large amounts of tough plant fibres.

> The Eoraptor existed during the early Triassic period some 228 million years ago and is considered to be one of the predecessors of all latter day dinosaurs.

Food habits

Carnivores

Meat-eaters (carnivores or theropods) need to have some way to get meat. Carnivorous dinosaurs usually had long, strong legs so that they could run quickly in order to catch their prey. They also needed large, strong jaws, sharp teeth and deadly claws so they could kill and then tear apart the prey. Good eyesight, a keen sense of smell, and a large brain to plan hunting strategies are also very important for successful hunting. Many of the carnivores (like Deinonychus, Coelophysis and Velociraptor) may have hunted in packs. So, social cooperation was necessary for a good hunt for some species. Animals that are primarily scavengers (animals that eat meat that they did not kill themselves) need very sharp teeth and strong jaws for tearing into less than prime cuts of meat, and breaking bones to get the nutritious bone marrow. Some dinosaurs were fish eaters. A few dinosaurs have been found with small, fossilized animals within their fossil, giving information about their diet. Some dinosaurs may have even been cannibals, eating their own kind.

Omnivores

Only a few of the known dinosaurs were omnivores (eating both plants and animals). Some examples of omnivores are Ornithomimus and Oviraptor, which ate plants, eggs, insects, etc.

Astonishing fact

The Corythosaurus was a crested duck-billed dinosaur which existed during the late Cretaceous Period around 80 million years ago.

Dinosaur behaviour

A lot can be said about the life of long extinct animals, such as the dinosaurs just by examining their bones. By looking at the fossils, scientists are often able to state what a given animal fed on, whether it was quadrupedal or bipedal, how fast it could move and many other things. What is still very hard to obtain from fossilized remains is evidence for the behaviour of dinosaurs. The knowledge is obtained from such remains as eggs, nests and skull fossils.

The most famous example of behaviour that has become known due to fossil material is parental care in Maiasaura, a hadrosaur from North America. By studying the nests found in Montana, palaeontologists were able to conclude that these hadrosaurs did take care of their young.

Evidence for social behaviour have also been found in the form of fossils-tracks of several sauropods travelling in the same direction have been found and interpreted as evidence for herding behaviour. Bone beds of hundreds of hadrosaurs and ceratopsians also indicate that some dinosaurs travelled in large herds.

> The largest carnivore dinosaur to have ever existed was the Spinosaurus.

Dinosaur behaviour

Birds are the living descendants of dinosaurs. Birds have another way to communicate that seems to have been shared by their dinosaur ancestors. Just as people recognize each other mostly by the way we look, birds and dinosaurs used feathers and probably, colours to recognize each other. In the last twenty years, many dinosaurs with feathers have been discovered. Birds use different coloured feathers for a variety of behaviours. They are used to attract mates, to identify individual members of a family or group, they are used to scare or fool attackers, and they are used to keep warm and dry. It seems likely that dinosaurs used their feathers for the same reasons.

Several dinosaur skeletons have been found with serious injuries, such as broken legs that have healed. This means that, while the injured dinosaur was unable to hunt for food, another dinosaur was bringing it something to eat. This is very complex social behaviour.

Fossil footprints are another way scientists learn about behaviour. These show that dinosaurs often travelled in large herds and in some cases even show how they hunted. And by studying the fossil remains of plants and the other animals that are found mixed in with dinosaur bones, scientists can create an even more detailed picture of dinosaur behaviour. As is evident, different types of fossils can tell a trained scientist many different things about the behaviour of a dinosaur. Bones, footprints, nests and many more bits and pieces of a dinosaur's life can create a big picture of life in the past.

DINOSAURS

Birds probably evolved from the Maniraptors, a branch of bird-like dinosaurs. In order to determine what animals birds evolved from, scientists use fossil evidence to trace the emergence of bird-like traits. Many Mesozoic era bird-like creatures have been found, some which are clearly dinosaurs.

The Archaeopteryx is one of the most famous and oldest-known fossil birds and dates from the late Jurassic period (about 150 million years ago).

It is now extinct. Although it had feathers and could fly, it had similarities with dinosaurs, including its teeth, skull and certain bone structures. Some palaeontologists think that Archaeopteryx was a dead-end in evolution and that the maniraptors led to the birds.

The first Archaeopteryx fossilized feather impression was found in 1860 in a limestone quarry in Germany. A year later, a much more complete fossilized Archaeopteryx was found at the same quarry. Impressions of its feathers and bone structure were quite clear. Many more have been found since for a total of seven.

Extinction

One of the great mysteries in science is the extinction of the dinosaurs at the end of the Mesozoic era some 65 million years ago. Who or what caused it is unknown and a subject of great debate.

Some of the theories proposed for dinosaur extinction have been:

The Asteroid Theory

One of the most well-known theories suggested for dinosaur extinction is the Asteroid Theory. In the 1980's the father-son team of Luis and Walter Alvarez discovered a layer of iridium in that period's rock layer. Iridium is rare on Earth, but abundant in meteorites. The duo suggested that a huge asteroid or comet hit the Earth at that time. The result of such an impact would be an enormous explosion that would throw dust clouds into the sky darkening the planet. Massive forest fires triggered by the hit, would add smoke to the sky. This would cool the planet causing the climatic changes observed.

A crater, now worn down and partly under the ocean, was found along the Mexican Yucatan Peninsula and its creation coincides nicely with the K-T boundary. NASA scientists estimate that the asteroid that made Chicxulub crater, as it is now known, would have been about 6 to 12 miles in diameter. The crater is about 130 miles across.

Not all scientists are satisfied with the Asteroid Theory, however. They point out the fossil record shows the dinosaurs were already in decline and the asteroid might just have been the final blow that finished off a population already weakened by some other factor.

Climate change

The climate of the Cretaceous period was tropical. Scientists know this because nearly one half of the plants in this time were tropical plants. Many scientists believe that at the end of the Cretaceous period the temperature dropped. If this drop in temperature is correct, many of the plants that the plant eating dinosaurs ate would die and thus many of the plant eaters would die as well. If the plant eaters died there would be nothing for the meat eaters to eat and they would eventually die out also. Plankton also seemed to decrease in number during the Tertiary period which could explain the death of the marine dinosaurs that fed on them. This popular theory just possibly could have caused the dinosaurs demise.

Deccan traps

Other scientists think the extensive volcanic activity in India known as the Deccan traps may have been responsible for, or contributed to, the extinction. However, palaeontologists remained doubtful, as their reading of the fossil record suggested that the mass extinctions did not take place over a period as short as a few years, but instead, occurred gradually over about ten million years, a time frame more consistent with massive volcanism.

Many herbivorous dinosaurs formed herds and like elephants today; the young ones were placed in the middle of the group, for protection.

Are they all dead?

Did any of the dinosaurs survive the extinction? Scientists have very rarely found bones of dinosaurs buried above the K-T Boundary end of Mesozoic era and beginning of Cenozoic era. A single Hadrosaur leg bone found in the San Juan Basin, New Mexico, might suggest that a small population of these dinosaurs survived as long as a half a million years into the following Paleocene era. However, it is also possible that the fossils in question, which are very few in numbers, were unearthed by some geologic event, then reburied at a higher level.

Occasionally, stories still appear about dinosaurs being found still alive today in some remote location of the world (for example, the legend of mok'ele-mbembe in Africa). While there are several famous fictional books like Arthur Conan-Doyle's The Lost World on this subject, there is no hard evidence that any dinosaur, other than the birds, their avian decedents have survived into modern times.

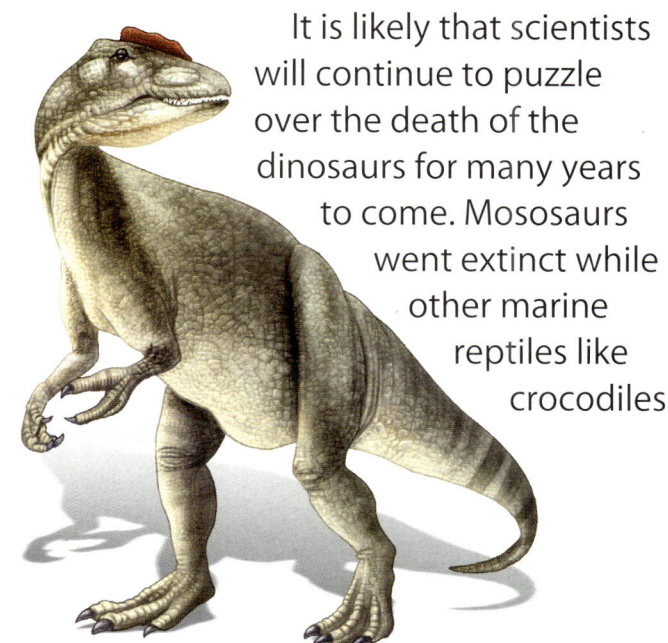

It is likely that scientists will continue to puzzle over the death of the dinosaurs for many years to come. Mososaurs went extinct while other marine reptiles like crocodiles are still around. If climate change is responsible why did the dinosaurs, creatures that lived in all kinds of conditions all over the planet, die when frogs, who are much more sensitive to temperature change, still survive today?

> **One of the smallest dinosaurs, the Compsognathus, weighing 3 kg with a speed of roughly 64 km per hour, could outrun an ostrich, the fastest living animal, with a speed of 8 km per hour.**

Dinosaur fossils

Dinosaur fossils have been known about for millennia, though their true nature was not recognized. The Chinese considered them to be dragon bones, while Europeans believed them to be the remains of giants and other creatures. The first dinosaur species to be identified and named was Iguanodon, discovered in 1822 by the English geologist Gideon Mantell, who recognized similarities between his fossils and the bones of modern iguanas. Two years later, the Rev William Buckland, professor of geology at Oxford University, became the first person to describe a dinosaur in a scientific journal — in this case Megalosaurus bucklandii, found near Oxford.

The study of these 'great fossil lizards' became of great interest to European and American scientists and in 1842 the English palaeontologist Richard Owen coined the term 'dinosaur'. He recognized that the remains that had been found so far — Iguanodon, Megalosaurus and Hylaeosaurus, had a number of features in common. So he decided to present them as a distinct taxonomic group.

> **First discovered in 1917 in Alberta Canada, Panoplosaurus is one of the best known of all armoured dinosaurs.**

Dinosaur fossils

(though much older bird-like footprints are known). Scans of the early flyer's skull now reveal that it came equipped with the complex brain that a modern bird requires for flight. Other studies reveal that feathered legs may also have helped it get off the ground.

> Dromiceiomimus resembled the modern day Emu of Australia, which is why it was named Dromiceiomimus which means 'Emu Mimic'.

In 1858, the first known American dinosaur was discovered in the small town of Haddonfield, New Jersey. The creature was named **Hadrosaurus foulkii**, after the town and the discoverer, William Parker Foulke. It was an extremely important find. Hadrosaurus was the first nearly complete dinosaur skeleton ever found and it was clearly a **bipedal creature**. This was a revolutionary discovery, as it had been thought by most scientists that dinosaurs walked on four feet like lizards.

Since then, the search for dinosaurs has been carried to every continent on Earth. This includes Antarctica, where the first dinosaur, a nodosaurid Ankylosaurus, was discovered on Ross Island in 1986.

New studies have also increased our knowledge about 150 million-year-old Archaeopteryx— immortalised as the missing link between birds and dinosaurs

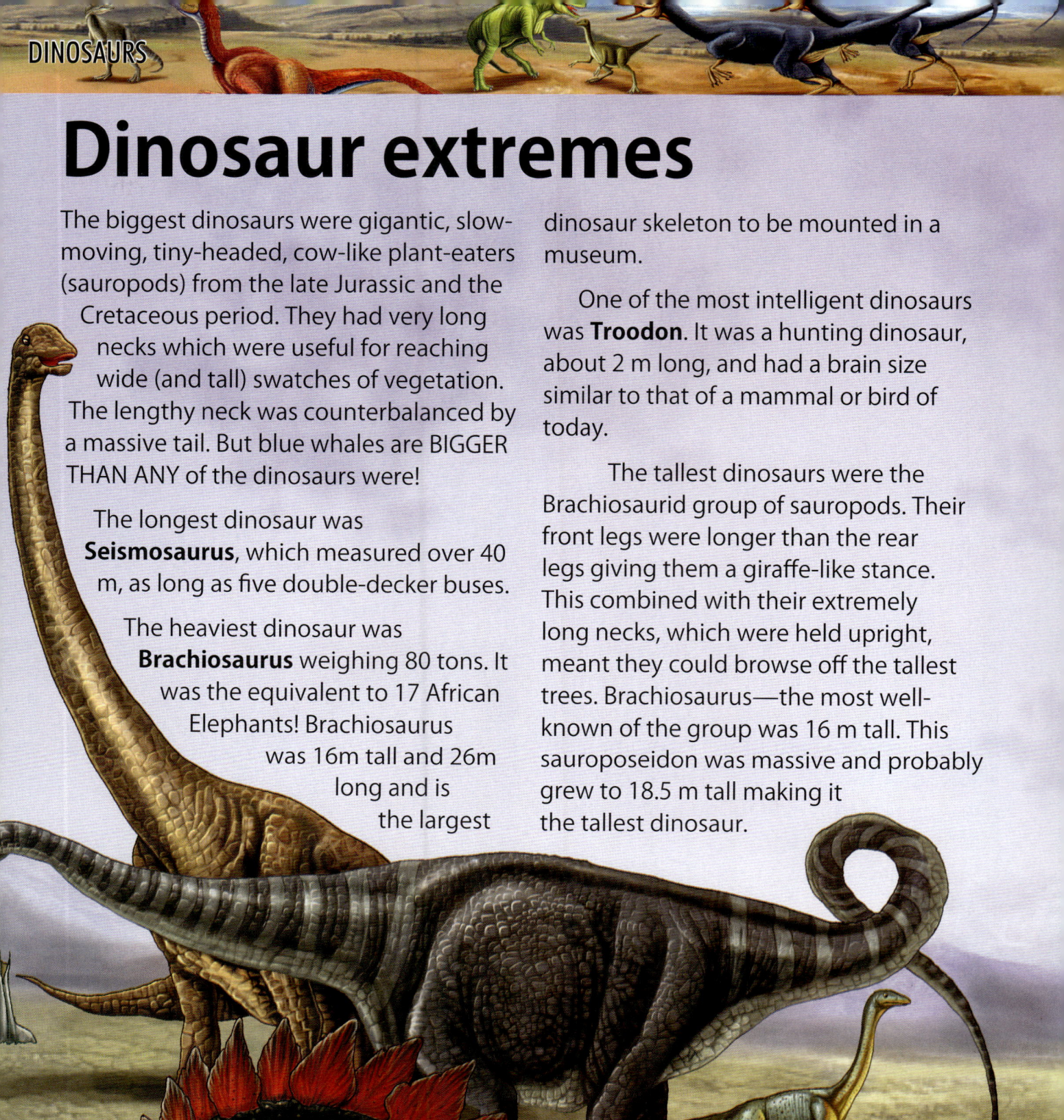

Dinosaur extremes

The biggest dinosaurs were gigantic, slow-moving, tiny-headed, cow-like plant-eaters (sauropods) from the late Jurassic and the Cretaceous period. They had very long necks which were useful for reaching wide (and tall) swatches of vegetation. The lengthy neck was counterbalanced by a massive tail. But blue whales are BIGGER THAN ANY of the dinosaurs were!

The longest dinosaur was **Seismosaurus**, which measured over 40 m, as long as five double-decker buses.

The heaviest dinosaur was **Brachiosaurus** weighing 80 tons. It was the equivalent to 17 African Elephants! Brachiosaurus was 16m tall and 26m long and is the largest dinosaur skeleton to be mounted in a museum.

One of the most intelligent dinosaurs was **Troodon**. It was a hunting dinosaur, about 2 m long, and had a brain size similar to that of a mammal or bird of today.

The tallest dinosaurs were the Brachiosaurid group of sauropods. Their front legs were longer than the rear legs giving them a giraffe-like stance. This combined with their extremely long necks, which were held upright, meant they could browse off the tallest trees. Brachiosaurus—the most well-known of the group was 16 m tall. This sauroposeidon was massive and probably grew to 18.5 m tall making it the tallest dinosaur.

Dinosaur extremes

The speediest dinosaurs were the ostrich mimic ornithomimids, such as **Dromiceiomimus** which could probably run at speeds of up to 60 km per hour!

The oldest dinosaurs known are 230 million years old and have been found in Madagasgar. As yet they have not been formally named. Before this Eoraptor, meaning 'dawn thief' had held the title at 228 million years.

Tyrannosaurus Rex looked the most ferocious of all the dinosaurs, but in terms of overall cunning, determination and its array of vicious weapons it was **Utahraptor** that was probably the fiercest of all. Utahraptor measured about 7 m, and was a very powerful, agile and intelligent predator.

Quetzalocoatlus with its wingspan of up to 13 m was probably the largest pterosaur and hence the largest flying creature of all time. Despite its size it weighed no more than 100 kg.

Astonishing fact

Not all the dinosaurs were enormous beasts. The Shanag, found in Mongolia, was about the size of a crow!

Pterosaurs were not dinosaurs.

Elasmosaurus was the longest plesiosaur at up to 14 m long. Half of its length was its neck, which had as many as 75 vertebrae in it (in comparison to 7-8 neck vertebrae in humans). **Elasmosaurus** had four long, paddle-like flippers, a tiny head, sharp teeth in strong jaws and a pointed tail. **Plesiosaurs** were not dinosaurs but were marine reptiles.

Some well-known dinosaurs

Tyrannosaurus Rex

No dinosaur list is complete without the mention of Tyrannosaurus Rex. It is one of the largest flesh-eating dinosaurs that ever lived. Fossil evidence shows that Tyrannosaurus was about 12 m long and about 15 to 20 ft tall. Its strong thighs and long, powerful tail helped it move quickly, and its massive 5 ft-long skull could bore into prey.

Tyrannosaurus Rex was a fierce predator that walked on two powerful legs. This meat-eater had a huge head with large, pointed, replaceable teeth and well-developed jaw muscles. It had tiny arms, each with two fingers. Each bird-like foot had three large toes, all equipped with claws (plus a little dewclaw on a tiny, vestigial fourth toe).

Scientists believe this powerful predator could eat up to 230 kg of meat in one bite. Tyrannosaurus Rex lived in forested river valleys in North America during the late Cretaceous period. It became extinct about 65 million years ago in the Cretaceous-Tertiary mass extinction.

Troodon

Troodon was a carnivore that lived in North America during the late Cretaceous period, about 74 to 65 million years ago.

Troodon was about 1.8 m long, 3 ft tall and probably weighed about 60 kg.

Troodon was one of the cleverest of all dinosaurs, having a large brain in proportion to its body weight. It was probably about as smart as a modern bird. Some scientists have even suggested that were it not for the Cretaceous-Tertiary extinction, Troodon may eventually have evolved human-level intelligence!

Maiasaura

The name Maiasaura means **Good Mother Lizard**, and was chosen in honour of the fact that it was the first dinosaur species discovered with clear and convincing evidence that it cared for its young. This includes the fact that fossils of baby Maiasaura show that the hatchlings' legs were not fully developed, and were incapable of walking, yet also show partially worn teeth, indicating that the adults brought food to the nest.

Maiasaura was a plant-eating dinosaur that lived in North America during the late Cretaceous period, about 80 to 65 million years ago.

Maiasaura adults were about 9.1 m long, and weighed 3 to 4 tons. The creature could walk on two or four legs, and had no obvious defences against predators except for its heavy muscular tail, and the fact that it lived in large herds (some herds many have consisted of as many as 10,000 individuals).

Argentinosaurus

Few if any land animals have ever lived that were as large as Argentinosaurus. Discovered in 1993 by two palaeontologists in Argentina, Argentinosaurus used its incredible size to protect itself from predators.

Argentinosaurus was an herbivorous sauropod dinosaur that is the largest and the heaviest land animal that ever lived. It lived in South America (its fossils were discovered in Argentina) during the Cretaceous period, around about 100 million years ago.

An adult Argentinosaurus measured about 36.6 m in length and weighed up to 100 tons. Its height was 70 ft or about the size of a six-storey building!

Giganotosaurus

The longest meat-eating dinosaur yet discovered is Giganotosaurus, which was 13.5-14.3 m long and weighed about 8 tons and stood 12 ft tall (at the hips). It walked on two legs, had a brain the size of a banana, and had enormous jaws with 8-inch long serrated teeth in a 1.8 m long skull. Giganotosaurus was a theropod from the mid-Cretaceous, living about 100-95 million years ago, toward the end of the Mesozoic Era, the 'Age of Reptiles'.

Giga-noto-saurus means 'giant southern reptile'. Its fossil was unearthed in Argentina in 1994.

Giganotosaurus lived about 95 million years ago, during the late Cretaceous period. This was about 30 million years before Tyrannosaurus Rex, which was among the last of the dinosaur species alive before the Cretaceous-Tertiary extinction 65 million years ago.

Iguanodon

Iguanodon is one of the most popular and most well-known of all the dinosaurs. Living on the Earth for tens of millions of years, Iguanodon was also one of the most successful dinosaurs.

Iguanodon was a relatively gentle plant-eater, despite its enormous size (twice as heavy as an elephant) and the scary-looking, foot-long spikes on the ends of its thumbs. It's believed that these spikes may have been a means of defence against carnivores or perhaps just a handy appliance for breaking open tough-shelled fruits.

Iguanodon lived in the early Cretaceous period, about 135-125 million years ago, toward the end of the Mesozoic. The supercontinent Pangaea was breaking up at that time, but Iguanodon managed to spread to all the continents except Antarctica.

Stegosaurus

Stegosaurus is one of the most famous dinosaurs and surely one that has embedded itself in popular culture. This large, armoured herbivore lived during the late Jurassic period in the lush forests that had been created by the high sea levels, warm climate and abundant rain. Fossils of Stegosaurus have been found worldwide, with the most specimens located in North America.

Stegosaurus was the largest of the family of herbivorous dinosaurs that shared a name with it, the Stegosaurs. It was around 10 m long, 2 m tall and weighed about three and a half tons. It had a broad, fan-shaped body, short columnar legs to support its weight, and a tiny head. One of the most commonly-cited features about Stegosaurus is the size of its brain. The famous comparison has been made between its brain and a walnut. Although, Stegosaurus wasn't exactly highly intelligent, it didn't exactly need it given the array of natural defences it possessed.

Stegosaurus had seventeen diamond-shaped bony plates running down the length of its back in two rows. These plates may have served a number of purposes. The first was to protect the back of the herbivore from predator attacks. The second was that they could have been used as a heat regulation device. The final possible function was display, either to confuse predators or to attract mates during courtship. The plates might have served all three of these functions, but scientists can only speculate with the fossils that are available to them.

Stegosaurus also had spikes at the end of its flexible tail. These spikes were up to 4 ft long and were used for protection from predators; they pointed to the sides of the tail.

Ankylosaurus

Ankylosaurus is a very famous armoured dinosaur. All other armoured dinosaurs belong to the class Ankylosauria, which gets its name from this dinosaur. These dinosaurs were the prehistoric tanks of their time.

During the time period that Ankylosaurus roamed the North American continent, a number of large dangerous predators also were on the prowl, including Tyrannosaurus. Ankylosaurus was a slow moving herbivore and needed protection from these hungry hunters. This protection came in the form of sharp spikes, and a long heavy hammer tail that could be used to break the legs of its enemies. Even the eyelids of Ankylosaurus were plated for protection.

Ankylosaurus had a beak and small teeth which it used to browse the large quantities of plants necessary to sustain a 3 to 4 ton body. It was the biggest and heaviest of the several ankylosaurid species and grew up to 10 m long.

Velociraptor

Velociraptor is probably one of the most famous dinosaurs that have ever lived. Velociraptor meaning 'swift seizer' is one of the small, predatory dinosaurs that lived about 70 million years ago during the Cretaceous period. About the size of a turkey, Velociraptors were covered with feathers and walked on two legs. Adults grew to about 2.07 m in length and weighed up to 15 kg.

Velociraptor was among the smartest dinosaurs, as calculated from their brain and body weight ratio. This made them very deadly predators. Velociraptor may have hunted in packs, perhaps attacking even very large animals.

Velociraptor walked on two slender legs; it was certainly among the fastest of the dinosaurs, considering its long legs and light weight. Velociraptor may have been able to run up to roughly 60 km/hr for short bursts.

Allosaurus

Allosaurus was one of the most powerful, fearsome and deadly dinosaur of the late Jurassic. Allosaurus was a large bipedal carnivorous dinosaur measuring up to 12 m long. It was named 'different lizard' because its vertebrae were different from those of all other dinosaurs. Until the Tyrannosaurs appeared 50 million years later, Allosaurus and its relatives were the largest predators to roam the Earth.

The powerful skull of Allosaurus was the perfect meat-eating machine. The jaws were large and massive, with serrated teeth designed for cutting meat. It probably overpowered its prey and used its massive jaw muscles; its large, powerful neck and head and its dagger like teeth to kill and eat its prey. These predators were widespread. They left their broken teeth near the bodies of many animals, showing where they had been.

The front limbs of Allosaurus were short but strong and the hands had three fingers each. Each finger had a sharply curved and pointed claw. It probably used its front limbs to capture prey and grab the flesh when feeding. The rear legs were large and powerful, built for both speed and agility.

Fossils found in Utah, North America suggest that Allosaurus may have lived and hunted in groups or packs. As a pack, Allosaurus would have had little difficulty hunting the largest dinosaurs of the time.

> **Astonishing fact**
>
> The largest dinosaur egg ever found was 30 cm in length and belonged to the Hypselosaurus.

Some well-known dinosaurs

Dinosaurs

Deinonychus

Although it was far from the biggest dinosaur of the Cretaceous period, Deinonychus was especially fearsome because of its speed, its presumed ability to hunt in packs, and the enormous, sickle-shaped claws on its hind feet that it used to rip apart larger dinosaurs. It is often described as one of the deadliest dinosaurs to have ever roamed the earth.

This was a quick and agile meat eating machine that grew in length to about 11 ft long and measure about 3 ft at the hips. Its most formidable weapon was the curved claws on its hind feet and it is from these claws that it gets its name, which means 'terrible claw'.

Deinonychus walked on two slender, bird-like legs; it must have been a fast runner, considering its legs and light weight. When it ran, it rotated its huge foot-claw upwards and ran on the other toes.

Utahraptor

Utahraptor was a carnivore that lived in North America during the early Cretaceous period, between about 132 and 119 million years ago. Its name was chosen in reflection of the fact that it was discovered in the Cedar Mountain Formation in Grand County, Utah.

Utahraptor was about 6 m long, about 6½ ft tall, and probably weighed around 700 kg. Its most formidable weapon was the huge curved claws on its hind feet, each close to one foot in length. These claws were used for slashing and ripping the prey. It had a relatively large brain and large, keen, eyes.

Utahraptor was a carnivore, a meat eater. It probably ate just about anything it could slash and tear apart. When hunting in packs, Utahraptor could probably kill any prey it desired.

Utahraptor walked on two slender, bird-like legs; it must have been a fast runner, considering its legs and light weight. When it ran, it rotated its huge middle-toe-claw upwards and ran on the other toes.

Test Your MEMORY

1. Who invented the name 'dinosaur'?

2. Name the three periods of the evolution of the dinosaurs.

3. Where did dinosaurs live?

4. What did dinosaurs eat?

5. When did the dinosaurs become extinct?

6. Name the most intelligent dinosaur?

7. Which dinosaur was the heaviest?

8. Write a few lines about Tyrannosaurus Rex.

9. Name the largest dinosaur that ever existed.

10. What does Giganotosaurus means?

11. When was the Iguanodon discovered?

12. Name a famous movie on dinosaurs.

Index

A

Ankylosauria 28
Archaeopteryx 16, 21
autotrophs 11

B

Brachiosaurid 22

C

carnivorous 4, 13, 29
ceratopsians 10, 14

D

duck-billed 6, 13

E

ecosystems 4
extinct 3, 7, 14, 16, 19, 24

H

Hadrosaurus 21

J

Jurassic 3, 5, 6, 7, 16, 22, 27, 29

N

nodosaurid 21

O

ornithopods 6

P

Palaeontologists 7, 9, 10, 14, 16, 18, 25
palaeontology 9
Pangaea 4, 5, 7, 26

plate tectonics 5, 7

S

sauropods 5, 6, 8, 10, 14, 22
Sauroposeidon 22
supercontinent 4, 5, 7, 26

T

theropods 13
Triassic 4, 5, 7, 12
Triceratops 6, 11